I0541952

0

Books authored by Mary-Eisa

A Love Story, Forgiveness, and Prayers

Finding God's Goodness

Love Puts Things Right
(is an expanded version of *Finding God's Goodness* with added chapters and notes.

Love Puts Things Right

The Path to Healing Abuse and Trauma

Mary- Eisa

Love Puts Things Right

This book is an Extended version of "Finding God's Goodness." (With added chapters and notes)

Unless otherwise noted, Scripture quotations are taken from the New Oxford Annotated Bible New Revised Standard Version copyright 1991 and The King James Version Bible.

Published by Ingraham Sparks, 2023

ISBN: Paperback: 9798-988-2990 5-9
ISBN: eBook: 979-8-988-2990-6-6
ISBN: Hardcover: 979-8-988-2990-7-3

Dedication

My gratitude goes out to my dear husband, who makes everything possible and fills every day with joy. I am so grateful for the preciousness of family, my children, my darling grandchildren, friends, and the gift of life for us all.

Blessings and gratitude to my spiritual teacher, Kavika, whom I am blessed to have known. My prayer is that this book reflects the true teachings of Love.

And to my dearest warrior friends of Prayer. Together, we prayed, and together, we shared, as together, we all loved.

Chapters

Part Two: Prayer Index

Prologue

The Seriousness of Abuse and Trauma

I wish I could write a book about how fortunate we are that abuse and trauma are not something prevalent in our society, but sadly, I cannot.

Americans live with the staggering figures that one in five have been sexually molested as a child, which is only one shocking statistic. A parent's beating will physically scar one in four children. One out of eight children will grow up after witnessing their mother being beaten. All of this leaves scars on the souls and hearts of the victims. Wars create children who have seen unthinkable acts, as well as soldiers who endure the trauma of war itself. In this environment, there are many broken spirits desperately seeking healing and relief from their pain. We have a mighty work to do to heal our society and fellow human beings.

Healing from abuse doesn't have one answer for everyone. I chose a spiritual path described in this book, *Love Puts Things Right,* and documented my journey to heal my broken soul. I chronicle how I found the peace of mind I was seeking through prayer and meditation. Therapy alone was not helping me to let go of the endless mind chatter and pain. I cannot tell anyone healing from trauma is easy because it is not; it can take years, even a lifetime, with relentless determination. My path was indeed spiritual, but because of my ancient studies, I had unknowingly become involved in the techniques now known through the study of neuro-cardiology, which is the study of the heart and brain. The Ancients, mystics, Indigenous, yogis, and Jesus all understood how the body metabolizes negativity; however, science had not yet caught up with the different functions of our miraculous self-regulating ability. It was unknown that the 40,000 cells within the heart include their own memory cells that can sense independently from the brain. We are now learning to use this miraculous power!

Scientists are now gaining a deeper understanding of the heart's memory cells through extensive research, uncovering previously hidden knowledge. The heart holds the key to our natural healing, providing a means to escape the pain of trauma and abuse.

In my pursuit of knowledge and personal growth, I have ultimately discovered the soothing balm of healing and tranquility for my troubled mind. With great joy, I now extend my journey to you, hoping it may offer some solace and support in your healing endeavors. However, it is essential to note that this book is not a substitute for professional medical aid. Always trust your intuition and never hesitate to seek and adhere to the guidance of medical professionals when necessary.

Chapter One

Introduction

Introduction

This story begins in a small community of maybe 200-300 people. A community where the sheriff and police force total one person, the sheriff, who was usually found sitting in the picture window of his living room watching his favorite ball game on TV. There wasn't a need for anything else because the primary crime wave was the local teens swiping the Shell gas station sign to use as a sled on the high, snowy New England hills. Oh, what fun! Behind the doors of each countryside home, you would find other families just living their lives. I grew up with my mother and new stepfather after my parents divorced. Then, I was barely two years old, and it was a harsh divorce, resulting in my sister deciding to live with her father. She later regretted losing her mother, but it was her choice, and her father and his family dearly loved her. We never saw each other again until we were in our teens. Living with my mother was challenging as she was what I would call emotionally problematic. I could never understand why she could not hug or express caring emotions. If triggered by fear, she could be explosive, but fortunately, she seemed much happier and calmer with her new husband. This is where my story starts as, behind closed doors, our home seemed happy and average, and in most ways, it was just that. My childhood became troubled because of my mother's problems. My dear mother could not mother a child or be physically affectionate. She didn't allow tears (a sign of weakness) and, after her divorce, caused me a terrible injury that would later require surgeries when my body had matured. In her way, she tried and loved as much as she could. We had a lovely home with everything for a good life, and I am grateful for that and everything we enjoyed.

I never believed or felt loved. I am sure the emotion of love was there, but I never felt the pleasure of being touched, hugged, or kissed. This left me feeling lost and aimless, constantly questioning what was wrong with me that prevented me from receiving love. As I reached my thirties, the physical toll of this emotional void began to manifest in my body. I found myself taking countless prescription medications to keep my heart and body free from the effects of severe allergies. My hearing, seeing, breathing, and heart were adversely affected. Finally, I realized I needed to act for my salvation and seek help before it was too late.

Now, joyfully later, as I navigate my much older adult life. My daily walks are accompanied by the refreshing touch of the crisp morning air, revitalizing all my senses. The sun's warm rays gently caress my skin, creating a comforting embrace. With each step, the earth beneath my feet grounds me, connecting me to the natural world. Today, during my walk, I am immersed in nature's beauty and carrying a small recording device to capture the sounds of nature intertwined with the echoes of my memories.

I have decided to allow my thoughts to wander and record my story. Memories flood my mind as I record them, ensuring they are etched in time to be later transcribed for this book. I can freely recall the transformative healing journey, guided by the first four essential steps that helped me enjoy today's solace and peace.

My initial attempt to understand my childhood involved diving into the realm of advanced Christian religious studies. Graduating from this study path marked a significant milestone, but it was only the beginning. For over a decade, I dedicated myself to prayer and aiding others on their spiritual journeys. Driven by an insatiable curiosity, I expanded my studies beyond Christianity, exploring other religions, ancient text, and their teachings. Seeking knowledge became a constant companion as I sought to uncover the healing wisdom that the ancients seemed to know so well. Through this exploration, I also began comprehending the universe's deeper essence.

I discovered that God's word did not solely reside within the confines of organized religions. Instead, it emanated from within, nestled deep within the heart. Love and its attributes of compassion, unconditional love, care, and kindness became the ultimate embodiment of God's presence, transcending any religious boundaries. I began learning to harmonize the heart and brain to heal my soul and allow my body to heal through its ability to self-regulate. A technique the ancients knew and taught, then were lost until the Dead Sea Scrolls and Nag Hammadi scriptures reveal their lost history.

This is the story of my quest to heal the wounds of trauma, to mend the tears that had plagued my soul. It is a journey that led me to uncover the goodness and happiness that we all deserve. In sharing this book, I want to share the healing that I discovered in my own life, hoping that it may also touch the lives of others and ignite a sense of joyous healing in their hearts.

Part two: The book contains the profound Sophie Letters. Sophie, a youthful European woman, endured a vicious assault, prompting my involvement as her mentor to aid in her recovery. I have carefully included two of my heartfelt letters to Sophie. My letters were written in the quiet solitude of my study, with the prayers to fill her with unwavering strength. With each chosen phrase and scripture, I wanted to empower and embolden her on her journey toward wholeness.

Part Three: These are beautiful prayers from my prayer book, along with added favorite quotes and poems.

Unlike many memoirs focused on trauma, "Love Puts Things Right" concisely explains the author's hardships, prioritizing a greater emphasis on the healing journey. This approach lends a distinct self-help book tone, as the author intertwines spiritual perspectives, often aligning the healing process with divine approval alongside practical and logical reasoning. The author's narrative is straightforward and candid, providing detailed accounts of her experiences and steps taken to find peace.
Online Book Club.org Review by Chinedum Chijoke

Beginnings

My Parents Divorce

My Parents' Divorce

Children will seek to find love in a million ways when love is withheld or lost. Sometimes, it might take their entire lifetime to come to peace with a painful past and find the lost parts of their childhood and identity. Understanding and accepting my parents' humanness became a near-lifetime journey. I wanted to uncover my authentic self, learn to trust again and move forward in peace through Love, Compassion, Kindness, and Self-Care.

We were a family that once enjoyed being together with relatives and friends constantly coming and going. Grandmothers who came and loved taking my sister with them to lunch, and a father who came home from work with delicacies hidden in his pockets waiting to be discovered. My sister enjoyed riding with her father on his motorcycle before supper—my habit of getting stuck against a wall when swinging too vigorously in my little rocking chair.

Our once vibrant family, filled with laughter and energy, was abruptly disrupted on a hazy late afternoon. On a day when the air felt heavy, my mother, driven by a new yearning, had decided to leave. She took only me with her, fueled by an unwavering determination to embark on a new chapter.

Uncertainty casts a shadow over our once blissful home. Our lives, once whole, were now shattered and could never again be fully repaired. The bittersweet scent of nostalgia filled the air as my sister, left behind, embarked on years of anguish. Meanwhile, I found myself on a perilous journey, facing daunting challenges brought upon by her departure and the unpredictable struggles with her behavior. Our family was broken.

Chapter One

A Beautiful Day!

A Beautiful Day!

Thank you, God, for this beautiful day.
The birds are singing,
Leaves are dancing in the gentle breezes,
The sun glows brightly,
As fluffy white clouds
drift divinely across the clear blue sky.
Oh, thank you for this glorious day.
So Be It!

Good morning!

Step into my new morning. As the sun rises, its golden rays paint the sky in a vibrant tapestry of pinks, oranges, and purples. The chirping of birds fills the air; it is a glorious new day.

I woke up early this morning, thinking I would get in my daily walk before the day's heat arrived. The new extreme weather, mainly after COVID-19, has been a change for both young and old. I am in the latter category, being one of those pesky boomers. Still, we were a hardy bunch rolling through beautiful times and times that were not, then, isn't that what life is all about, moving through whatever is placed before us?

Sitting up in bed, I begin my day with prayers to the universe. I like to set my intention for the day.

Good Morning, Universe; I thank you for this day and the opportunity to share it all with you. As I go about my day, I pray to be your instrument. May I succeed in all the tasks before me and see everything as a gift from you. Please help me keep my eyes open and only on you as I go safely about this day. Amen.

After finishing breakfast, I left to begin my morning walk, grabbing my mug of tea. It will be another warm and humid day, so I am starting earlier than usual. As I make my way down the wooded path, the coolness of the early hours lingers. The air was crisp, and I could see only a blanket of solid white clouds. The clouds were blocking the morning sun, adding almost an eeriness to the day, with white mist falling around me. As a child, I would rush into the forest to feel the whisper of a gentle breeze blowing through the pines and smelling their spicy aromas. As I walked through the forest floor, brushing my shoes through the pine needles, roots, broken branches, and vibrant leaves dyed in many colors. The forest was my place to untie the school knots and escape each day's pettiness. Every day, I would run into a world that was a living, breathing, and sensuous cosmic organism. A spiritual character imparted by nature that I realized was part of my spiritual life. I felt a deep connection with everything around me. I could sense the vibrant energy and the impending storm approaching. The trees and animals seemed to be sending out their warnings; amazingly, I could understand their messages.

Know that the whole world is a mirror; in each atom are found a hundred blazing suns. If you split the center of a single drop of water, a hundred pure oceans spring forth. A thousand Adams can be seen if you examine each particle of dust.
–Mahmud Shabistan

As I began my usual morning walk, I considered sharing my thoughts to support other individuals with emotionally vulnerable families. With a recorder in hand,

I wandered down a meandering path. The crisp morning air filled my lungs, mingling with the scent of freshly bloomed flowers as I strolled along the familiar route. The gentle rustle of leaves and the gentle chirping of birds provided a soothing backdrop to my contemplations. In due time, I will determine how to transcribe these recorded reflections later. But for now, I embrace the solace and tranquility of my walk.

I have heard it said that the dance of life could begin at eighty, but I think that perhaps it starts at the very beginning. The day we are born and meet for the first time, the two people who created us. Our bonding begins in those very first moments when our physical journey as a family takes its first steps. My parents have been gone now for many years. Our years were troubled, but even so, they were filled with many joys, and I dearly wish we could have had more time to share in which we might have understood and loved more together. Jesus said, "Honor thy mother and father," and he did not mention any exceptions. My parents were naturally part of a different group from mine, having had their generation's experiences and social values. Every generation seems to have its objective and destiny, striving collectively to attain its intention. I must assume that each generational period is needed to progress to the next step. They must each fulfill their promise and script to prepare the next generation to follow. Today, we stand on our ancestors' shoulders, blessed to have the advanced technology to learn from history and move our generation forward to the subsequent (hopefully) higher spiritual advancement. I believe we are doing just that.

My parent's generation had a turbulent history, with wars, depression, and many restrictions on humanity. Today, we still face some old encounters with the new added challenges of our technologically vastly growing world. Their world and life must have progressed with great trepidation, living through all the economic shortages and fear of a country at war. Their generation has earned my tremendous respect and gratitude.

If we must believe in a fallen world of fallen souls, then our Bible is critical for giving us the rules and laws to guide our behavior and lead us to a better place in our soul's evolution, *where we can attain the measure*

and full stature of Christ.
Eph 4:13

Similarly, my thoughts effortlessly glide to our constitution, written in a biblical tone to suggest the rules and laws we need to flourish peacefully in an orderly republic. While we, as individuals, strive to become higher spiritual beings, our country also seeks to reach higher levels of consciousness so that we can live together in peace with one another and the world.

Our constitution attempts to guide us in resolving our differences through communication, our laws, and the will to respect each other's many differences in our struggle to live together in harmony. Both individually and as a country, everything and everyone appears to go a few steps forward and then a few steps backward— the ebb and flow of people, government, and the planet.

It always amazes me how everything works together to create almost a marvelous matrix for us as individuals and our world. This is the place where we live and raise our families. Some call it *our grand school.*

As I walked along, I noticed that my mind

was again wandering as it so loves to do, and smiling at myself, I returned to the present, placing an awareness of the birds singing in chorus throughout the woods. When I listen to the melodic tunes of a singing bird, I perceive it as a divine prayer. These avian messengers traverse the vast expanse of the universe, their melodic songs resounding through the heavens and the earth. Perched upon lofty trees, they share their wisdom through enchanting melodies. They will reveal their profound insights if we listen to their harmonies. At night, an owl choruses a melody of hoots as a meditation on love. If we listen, the voice of nature will speak to us and sing us a most miraculous song.

As the rest of my walk continued, I felt quiet within my soul and reverence for an important task ahead of me. The previous night, I received a phone call asking me to write and help a young woman in a terrible crisis. It was hoped my life experiences could be helpful to her. The impending need reverberated through the air.

Yet, every experience endured holds the potential to aid another's journey. Assisting Sophie in finding her sanctuary of peace would be a profound privilege. I'm convinced that every encounter happens for a reason, and with divine guidance, I feel blessed to be part of this endeavor.

As I continued, a glimmer of hope sparked within me. I prayed that this work could potentially profoundly and significantly bring solace to others.

All the rivers run into the sea, yet the sea
is not full;
unto the place from which the rivers
come,
thence they return again.
　　　—The Bible, Ecclesiastes

.

Nothing is more essential to prayer than attentiveness.
–Evagrius the Solitary, fourth-century monk and ascetic.

Chapter Two

Going Deeply Within

Going Deeply Within

Several weeks have passed, and I felt a quietness within my soul. My past is now just memories of a life lived long ago and no longer carries feelings of pain or regret. I believe life should not hold any regrets; it should be just the passing of time and learning experiences.

Today was new, and I could feel the early morning weather cooling as the air had a definite chill. The clouds moved, exposing the sun to new splendor and inviting light and warmness through the umbrella of speckled leaves overhead. The apricity of my shawl covering my body and shoulders feels lovely as I wrap myself more tightly while continuing my walk. I have sent my first letter to Sophie. The wings of mail are carrying it along to reach her in her remote home soon, so far away from here. I can't help but pray for a day when the thoughts of harming another soul do not even pass through another person's mind. As I walk along, I recall the terrible incident with my mother. After my mother's divorce, there were some very difficult months. My mother was alone with me during what must have been a fearful time for her. She planned to remarry as soon as the war was over, and of course, that would depend on him coming home safely. I was not quite two years old on this particular day, and we were alone in a room. I was making a real fuss, wanting to go home. Divorce was not something I could understand. My carrying-on was not what she wanted to hear as she exploded with her fist and a bottle breaking in the center of my face. There was such force with her adrenalin heightened that it wasn't until months later that everyone began noticing my nose wasn't healing. The bridge was damaged, and the nose cartilage and tissue no longer developed as the face matured. The tissue seemed pulverized from the forceful impact of severe trauma.

In my situation, the trauma caused irreversible tissue, cartilage damage, and loss of function as trauma activates the immune system and alters stem cell behavior. I thought of my nose as *frozen in time* the moment it happened. Perhaps, in some ways, my spirit was also frozen in time.

My mother took me by train to her mother's house for care until she was forced to admit me to the hospital. The doctor's queries continued with many questions regarding what happened; however, my

Grandmother stuck to her story that I had just fallen. Some things might have helped then, but the doctors needed to know the facts of what happened. Later, when my face appeared outwardly healed, my grandmother returned me to my mother, which had to be more emotional trauma. My father was never told what happened, as my sister and grandmother decided to keep the secret.

After my parents divorced and the war ended, my mother married the man she had been waiting for while he was serving in the Navy. Her new husband had studied to be an Episcopalian priest before being drafted into WWII. His family was very spiritual and a blessing to us both. I thought of him as our *True North*. He loved my mother very much, and their love was expressed constantly, as anyone could see her glow and calmer behavior. They were very wrapped up in each other and she seemed to be able to show affection to him. Their marriage began our new family life. Together, we would all create the ebb and flow of our lives. I believe my mother and stepfather, whom I would soon call daddy, did their best to support me despite the challenges I would face. I felt my new Daddy was trying to build a better life for my mother and me. He knew that she had severe problems and was insecure, perhaps he believed that she would overcome her emotional disabilities through love and kindness. My mother was noticeably calmer and genuinely happy when he entered our lives. They were very much in love.

During my mother's lifetime, she never talked about what happened to me and seemed unable to face it. My mother and my grandmother even tried to create a story that the damage was from a birth defect that showed up as I grew older. Then suddenly, they needed a story, a carefully crafted narrative that would allow my sister to come and live with us. It had to be convincing enough to appease my father, who would undoubtedly be shocked to see my face, that wasn't the same face he would have remembered.

He would have insisted on visiting if my sister had lived with us. The weight of that situation was palpable in the air. However, there was still the unresolved issue of my mother denying my father the court-granted visitation rights. In response, he refused to pay child support. I'll never know how these two parties would have resolved their problems since my sister did not stay,

In politics, they claim it isn't the crime but the cover-up that causes the biggest problem. It can also be that way in families, but it is always about fear. The fear of others knowing what had happened to my face. However, my stepfather announced he would never lie and would tell the truth if asked. He might have wisely recognized that the truth would be uncovered if anyone questioned medical doctors. Consequently, my sister had to leave and return to her father.

My grandmother never talked about if my mother had a bad temper; however, there must have been evidence of this as a child. These problems usually go back to childhood and are often part of a pattern of family dysfunction. I vividly remember my grandmother with her warm, affectionate hugs and genuine aura of care. However, delving into her past, I discovered that she was once known for her tenacious and determined nature, earning her a challenging reputation. My grandfather (her husband) suddenly left one day and never returned. Their marriage obviously had difficulties, leaving my grandmother with three young children who continued to express affection for their father. They often spoke of their excitement when he returned home from work as they eagerly crawled all over him with childhood glee. I suspect that my mother's problems might be connected to her mother, the loss of her father, the betrayal of her first husband, and possibly even further back to her grandmother.

Do we inherit these problems through our DNA or learn these behaviors from our experiences? I don't know if it's nature or nurture. I do know, however, that we have the power not to accept others' behaviors as our own.

Life presents us with obstacles, giving us the choice to grow or retreat. It ultimately depends on us. People say that God never gives us more than we can handle, but there were times when I felt the weight was too much to bear. When our burden feels overwhelming, it can help to find solace in the shared weight of the struggles carried by others. Life is a symphony of laughter and tears, harmoniously blending. Perhaps this is how we learn to appreciate joy when it enters our lives. I had to keep going and deal with everything the best I could since what was done was done.

When I reached the age to start school, I faced the harsh reality of bullying and cruel name-calling. However, despite the hurtful words and actions, I persisted and advanced to the next grade level each year. Amidst it all, I found solace in becoming a Brownie and forming a deep bond with Elizabeth, a dear friend I first encountered at church.

My early years of Sunday school were spent in a lovely Episcopalian church, where my new daddy sang regularly in the church choir. Sitting with my Sunday school friends and seeing him singing behind the elaborate choir rail in his distinguished robe was divine. He had a beautiful, deep voice. I stood in the gathering feeling immensely proud. Around the age of eight, we moved to the country, where I attended a unitarian church, as it was the only church in our small country setting. Our home was remotely situated on a slight hill in front of acres of meadows and forest. Every summer morning, I was delighted to run through an open field sprinkled with an array of wildflowers and where a tractor each spring plowed to create a large section where the season's garden crops were planted. Rows of garden beans and tomato plants covered the ground in color while vegetables showered the land with all of nature's abundance. I snatched juicy tomatoes and crisp cucumbers from their vines to fill my pockets and carry them into the wood.

"I do not know how to distinguish between our waking life and a dream. Are we not always living the life that we imagine we are? Fear creates danger, and courage dispels it." –Henry David Thoreau.

Beyond the open meadow of our home was a simple path to enter the glorious, woodsy-scented forest. Partway into it was a stream where I would sometimes sit to observe cleverly woven dams created diligently by the architecture of beavers. Squirrels, rabbits, deer, moose, and raccoons ran around freely, with even occasional sightings of black bears. It was a paradise for the animal kingdom, where butterflies of all colors covered the countryside lavishly— a world where I became attuned to the invisible depths of life that surrounded us. A perfect Winnie-the-Pooh hundred-acre wood in our backyard and cosmos where the earth nurtures its seeds for the next season of maturing growth, and a child can wander and find adventure in a land that will seem of magical enchantment. Here, I found my first spiritual awakening as I tuned into the magic of the forest and animals. I could feel the universe's spirit within everything, and I was one with everything.

Earth's crammed with heaven,
And every common bush afire with God; But
only he who sees takes off his shoes….
—Elizabeth Barret Browning

In school, I learned academics, and in this woodsy exploration, I learned about the balance and harmony of the whole of creation—an awakening of God in everything and me.

The creation of a thousand forests is in one acorn. –Ralph Waldo Emerson

While I loved the woods and gardens, I was still very curious about my birth father while growing up. You can take the child away from the father but can't take the father out of the child. My mother didn't want to discuss anything about him. My stepdad was lovely, but I naturally wanted to know more about the person who helped create me. I decided to fill in all the missing blanks in my mind. I wanted to feel a sense of connection with him, and around the age of nine, I created my own story and told my friends he was a famous writer who traveled the world. I began my creative narrative by saying that he was very famous, like Earl

Stanley Gardner. That explained why we never saw him, and no one would recognize his name as he wrote under a pen-de-plum. It was a lovely story, and I felt so good that he now seemed real with an identity. If people hadn't seen him visiting me, it would have been because he was famous and traveling. It was all so logical and made me feel happy. Forgetting, of course, it was a small town and there was such curiosity about my missing father that my mother quickly learned of the story. She thought it was very funny but informed everyone that my father wasn't famous or a writer. He was a mechanic, often called a grease monkey. Trying to picture someone covered in grease didn't create a very nice image in my mind. I wasn't sure I wanted that image to be my father, and I eventually learned he was not even a mechanic. Her wounds with my father were deep and unyielding.

If prayer is pure and untainted,
Surely, that holy breath
That rises from your lips
Will join with the breath of heaven
That is always flowing
Into you from above …
Thus, that part of God
Which is within you
Is reunited with its source.
—Hasidic master

Chapter Three

Healing Begins

Healing Begins

I love to fill my thoughts with reminders of God's love as I walk along wooded paths and become aware of the sounds of rocks crushing and skittering away from my shoes, creating tumbling and crunching noises. The sounds of the world were everywhere: the birds singing, the wind in the trees, the woodpecker hammering away, rat-a-tat-tat, and the sounds of traffic moving along in the distance. The sounds fill our ears and direct us to pay attention instead of just looking.

To listen from our hearts is a precious time when we can form a new discipline and pay attention to our surrounding universe. It is a time to let go of everything our minds create without the denseness of ego and feel the being-ness part of the natural world untouched by human action.

If God created the universe to be known, then I wonder that he must have made the heart capable of feeling him beyond all our senses.

That which God said to the rose,
And caused it to laugh in full-blown
beauty,
He said to my heart,
And made it a hundred times more
beautiful.
–Jalaluddin Rumi

Fall is a magical time when most leaves have fallen, creating a carpet of color everywhere, preparing the trees for a season of rest, and fulfilling their life cycle. It is when the sun sprinkles through porous shimmering leaves casting a mist of jeweled light.

For God gave us a spirit not of fear but of power and love and self-control.
Timothy 1:7

As I continued my stroll, the world's music seemed to fill the air. Occasionally, there were the honking sounds of wild geese flying overhead. At the same time, squirrels seemed busy scampering about. Such enterprising fellows with bushy tails that fluttered as they darted here and there. In the distance, I could hear the chirps and cackles of a woodpecker busy pecking away to create his new home and seeking food. Like a diligent carpenter, this small bird works earnestly while dedicated to its goals. Unlike most people, he focuses entirely on his aim and has no other thoughts. I could barely see its tiny redhead bobbing busily above the branches of trees from far away. The woods are alive with every sound, color, and melody possible.

As I walked along enjoying the day, I suddenly remembered a spiritual teaching that when life takes something from us, it returns something else to us. We could call it a trade, perhaps. The woods and my awakening of nature were my gift or trade, filling a vast abyss life had created. When listening to the sounds of nature, you begin to feel included as part of everything around you. The universe has opened a new door in my life. It was a gift of awakening to the spirit through the wonders of God in nature.

The heat of the mug is warming my hands while the spices tickle my throat. The added extra black pepper and cloves are spicy and delightful. I decided to enjoy the morning clouds as they are just mystical. It is incredible that no matter what happens, everything is always perfect. I have no regrets as I realized everything in my life moved me forward to the next step and the person I am today. I like that person who has learned to accept whatever life hands us, let go of fear, and surrender to Love.

As I continued to reflect on my journey, I couldn't help but remember how much my mother's illness affected my childhood. I tried not to think about it because her problem, often referred to as IED (intermittent explosive disorder), was awful for me and also devastating to any person and their family. It is emotionally draining to be a child of a parent with any personality disorder, which is also difficult for everyone around them. When triggered, the person suddenly has impulsive, violent behavior without conscious thought. When this behavior becomes repeated, it becomes labeled a disorder. New studies outlined in Christiane Northrup, MD, in the book titled Dodging Energy Vampires, show that.

people who lack empathy and compassion are not created through problems in society or necessarily from childhood trauma but are born with a thinner membrane in the brain cortex that appears to be related to their lack of empathy. It can behave in many forms: violent outbursts, temper tantrums, narcissistic disorder, anxiety, attention deficit, bipolar, depression, and schizophrenia. It all begins with an overreactive fight response to anything that seems threatening as the underlying cause, which is always fear.

Fear is a natural emotion necessary to protect and keep us aware of any harm that could happen to us. The fight-or-flight response is essential for survival. However, this dysfunction is without everyday reasoning or control. My family's behavior problems appeared as possibly perpetuated through the family's nurturing and genetic predisposition. Dysfunctional behavior comes in many forms and flavors; however, its commonality is that it is always perpetuated by fear. People have asked me if the person with these disorders has any remorse, and it has been my experience that they do not, especially not in my situation.

Abuse seems to be acted out without considering the consequences for others. I have observed that people can often easily rationalize their behavior with self-created excuses: It wasn't that bad, it didn't matter, or it was all someone else's fault. However, having certain personalities or tendencies in our genes does not mean we must suffer from any disorder or personality trait. We can change that through our determination.

We can change our inherited personality traits through focused intervention and life-changing experiences.

Prayer and forgiveness can be that constant work of intervention.

A wandering road was traveled, To reach a new end.
The end became the new beginning, And this beginning was all bright and new.

I married right after high school and wish I could say I married wisely. Still, a child who has gone through a traumatic, abusive experience often will marry into another abusive situation, as I did. At the same time, my parents tried in their minds to give me a normal childhood and help me through everything that happened. But still, in my heart, I had accepted abuse as part of my life because it was part of my life and the part that was never addressed.

The much later reconstructive surgery gave me a better chance at life, but I do not think anyone was aware of all the emotional scars and trauma buried deep within my soul. The psychological damage was so deep because of what my mother did, and her being emotionally unavailable plunged the wounds deeper. I seemed to blow whichever way the wind blew me, accepting things as they were. My spirit seemed broken. I wanted to admire the man I married. However, time soon proved he was extremely narcissistic and enjoyed doing precisely as he pleased, especially getting away with it. He was like a train, while I felt like the track he ran on. There were good times and bad times, but it would take a strong woman to be married to him, and that strength was not mine. He would keep acting immaturely and speaking negatively about everything until he got what he wanted. Tantrums instantly stopped once he achieved his goal. It was apparent he had years of this selfish practice and success during his childhood; after thirteen years, I left the marriage in a severely deteriorated physical and mental condition. I was running for my life.

Finding the person God desired me to be would take years of healing work and a very big shovel. … **So the work begins.**

It would be years before I would completely recognize the depth of damage I had suffered through my childhood and later in my former marriage. It was soul-deep, and inside, I felt confused and broken. The human mind is more delicate than we think. It stores all our trauma and emotional conflict deeply inside our subconscious and body. Every cell in our body knows the impact of the traumas we have experienced. I seemed unable to fight back with an instinctive fear of another fist or attack. There, hiding within my entire body, was my brokenness.

I worked studying and getting help to rebuild my life. I started feeling much stronger and reached out to my family with disastrous results.

There were many challenges within our family, particularly concerning my sister, who was deeply disturbed as a result of growing up without her mother. Even though she requested to be with her father in divorce court, she insisted that being almost four years old was too young to make that decision. However, she made such a fuss in court that the judge felt she was old enough to decide. As her grandmother often said, my sister was extremely strong-willed. Of course, wanting both parents was natural; however, my sister, our mother, and the court changed that for both of us.

Lying doesn't create a truth; it's still a lie.

When I was about twenty, I finally met my father again. I witnessed how much he loved my sister and saw that he and his family tried to give her a good life. However, she was strong-minded about having her mother, too. She insisted I needed to share everything I had and that sharing was all she wanted to do, but her actions said otherwise. They said she wasn't interested in sharing her life with me and wanted both parents.

Mark Twain: *"Action speaks louder than words but not nearly as often.*

I hadn't realized how emotionally disturbed my sister became, so much so that I shouldn't ever trust her. To put everything all mildly, it was a real pickle. I was emotionally wounded because I grew up with my mother, while my sister was emotionally wounded because she didn't grow up with her mother. It was incredibly challenging to comprehend everything, especially considering my sister's striking beauty and the adoration she received from our father and his side of the family. Understanding the depth of her resentment proved to be difficult for me. I could only evaluate the situation from my perspective and draw from my own life experiences; I could empathize but could not fully grasp her unique experiences. While I was quiet and known for being very reserved, my sister was very outgoing and able to express love and emotions easily. Our personalities were complete opposites of each other.

However, her bitterness caused deceitful actions, sending my life spiraling into an excruciating depression that felt like falling into a dark void called the *dark night of the soul*. I was in a deep, dark place with so much heartbreak and pain that I could no longer see a path in my life. I forgot about all the good things and could only feel pain.

I no longer wanted to be on this earthly plane. I had given up on everyone and everything in life. I wanted no more from life and decided everyone was right; as my sister so cruelly said, "I was worth nothing." They had won. My desire to leave this world was so intense and buried in total anguish that I sincerely meant my words; "I wanted to die.' My brokenness was lost in these moments of despair and surrender. Within moments of God's heavenly time, I was suddenly standing beside my body, looking down at it, still lying on the sofa.

Yes, the controversial near-death experience that I can only say in one moment, I was here, and the next, I was there. Impossible to explain in words. In almost the same celestial instant, I sat at a table in a serene place with a person I decided must be my guardian angel. There was such stillness and surrounding peace that I wanted to curl up and stay there forever in perfect slumber and never leave. Nonetheless, I had been brought there for a purpose. I was shown My Book of Life in the Akashic Records. This divine presence wanted to convey a profound message: the goodness I had accomplished surpassed any perceived missteps that burdened my heart. God is not as hard on us as we are on ourselves.

From the beginning of my life, people's words and actions made me feel small and lesser than them. I had accepted their words into my heart and suffered from something not mine. My family was complex and filled with emotionally destructive patterns. I would need to realize my self-worth and see myself as the perfect child of our creator. Yep, all those lovely words we read in books and hear spoken in church, well, now I needed to take them into my heart, believe, and *live* them. I needed to believe in myself as a child of God and not the destructive words of others. In Jesus's words …

Do not give what is holy to dogs, and do not throw your pearls before as wine, or they will trample them underfoot and turn and maul you. Matthew 7:6

While that script sounds harsh, it is pretty much what happened. Since my life cycle was unfinished, I needed to return to finish my life. There was no roadmap or guidance, only the words to *let it all go.*

I needed to move above all this. I would have to figure everything out for myself. I had experienced a pathway through the veil and found that we are but a speck, constantly being watched, cared for, and loved. Jesus reminds us.

Those who say, "I love God, and hate their brothers or sisters, are liars; for those who do not love a brother and sister, whom they have seen, cannot love God, whom they have not seen. The commandment we have from him is this: Those who love God must also love their brother and sister. 1 John 4:20

I began a path to study everything I could, seeking help, studying different religions, books, and texts, and finally coming to a place that fits my soul. I accidentally (or since I believe there are no accidents, I divinely found) the School of Christianity. They were very open and warm to prayer; love was most important. I graduated from their school with a two-year advanced religious studies degree. The Course of Miracles was also a program I loved and studied while moving on to become part of the ministry in prayer for over a decade.

During those early years, I created my healing journal and recorded my four steps to heal.

My first actual physical and mental healing steps began with the following steps.

My Four Steps.

These are the four steps I used for my healing.

1. Healing Journal.
2. Accept the Experience.
3. Let go of any Judgments.
4. Surrender and Forgiveness.

My Healing Journal.

My first step to healing, when I began my healing journal, was writing the remembrances of my childhood and marriage. Putting it all on paper and reading it in black and white gave it a new animateness. I could witness the action in words, place the people in context, and see their patterns more clearly. Sometimes, through words, I could even feel their pain, and also my own. My journal began my journey to healing, and I gained great insight through it. The experience opened my eyes to the complexities I was dealing with and motivated me to seek assistance from a professional in order to gain a deeper understanding of my family dynamics and marriage. I delved into extensive research and attended various classes to gain insights into the intricacies of human behavior and enhance my knowledge about personality disorders.

At first, I wrote on a simple piece of paper and later started to put things together in small notebooks. I began by noting everything I could remember from my earliest memories and continued writing up to my last memory. Sometimes, the writing was small when I felt peace; other times, the written words became larger and firm as anger was felt. Writing everything down and feeling the words while recognizing their impact on me was essential. It helped me see the innocence of others. It took me over a year to complete. Whenever I felt inspired, I would document my emotions and observations.

My writing clearly showed that my feelings of being undervalued and unloved were a pattern in my life. I continued to attract people who continued these patterns, as like attracts like. Those feelings of low self-esteem, whether meant or intended, were causing my pain and suffering. I knew it would continue until I healed that part of myself. Ultimately, only the final words scribbled in my journal truly mattered. *Let it all Go.* They represented the present moment, while all the rest was just the past. An incident I experienced with my mother while I was in high school left a massive hole in my heart. I wrote details in my journal and with tears afterward. I could never comprehend why my mother was physically absent yet emotionally distant, leaving a void in my life that echoed with silent solitude.

On an early winter morning, the car I was traveling to high school slid on the icy road and flipped over. It was an old car, years before seatbelts, that would have prevented us from being thrown through the convertible roof, killing a student and friend. My stepfather picked me up from the hospital while Mom was at work and asked to see me before my stepfather took me home. When I approached her, tears suddenly ran down my cheek, and she quickly pushed me away. Tears were never acceptable. At the same time, my eyes caught my stepfather's face, looking sadly down. Back at home, I was noticeably shaken and covered with cuts and bruises and heard him quietly telling her I needed her while she answered, "I know, but I can't, I just can't." So, he comforted her.

A few days later, it rained hard. Whenever I heard of a funeral, it always seemed to rain that day. On this day, it rained very hard. I wondered if it was God's way of crying and trying to wash everything clean.

My mother was emotionally unable, and the man I married also could not appreciate another person's feelings or emotions. Their lack of feeling and caring was the life I knew and was familiar with. As long as we remain unhealed, we continue to attract similar people into our lives. I realized I needed to stop inviting these individuals into my life to break this cycle. The focus wasn't on categorizing them as right or wrong; they existed in their truth and served as mirrors, guiding me toward areas where healing was necessary and pointing out their need for healing.

Nevertheless, trying to hold onto these family members, hoping for a different outcome, was a form of co-dependency. It was my need for family love and affection. While this would be natural for anyone, it was time to close unhealthy chapters in my life.

Through my journal, I realized the necessity of going back and seeing the complete picture of my life I had carried in my heart every day. Then, I found it effortless to perceive and release all the drama. The only thing that truly existed was the present moment, as the past had already passed and vanished. It had no power to harm me anymore. It was never genuine, merely a deceptive portrayal of the dramatic events in my life that never truly defined me.

Albert Einstein once said, *"The distinction between past, present, and the future is only a stubbornly persistent illusion."*

It is something that is perceived through our perception that contradicts reality. As a young child, I was once frightened when I saw a man standing in our hallway in the middle of the night. It was freestanding coat rack draped with a scarf and hat in the hallway's darkness. To me, it appeared as if a man was standing there. Something perceived to me as true but was not true. If you identify with anything that is not valid, you are moving from what is true to the illusion of something that is not true. Our dramas are also not us.

Many years later, I thought about doing a burning bowl ritual to let go of the past. My spiritual advisor suggested I could instead share my journal by *paying it forward*. It was a painful journal, but after serious consideration, I decided my journal might have value in helping someone else. Others had also suffered through unhappy childhoods and family, and some much more than I and could benefit from reading my experience. I did a burning bowl celebration, which was a rewarding celebration. I added several incense cones to the flames, giving everything wonderful flaming hues of color and fragrance. However, I was aware that the ceaseless babble would persist until I brought about a change. Sharing tales that are even more heartrending than mine proved to be beneficial; it allows us to bring attention to all these circumstances. Then in the morning, the divine light of the universe reveals itself. Even the faintest lights will extinguish the darkness; Yeshua reminded us,

"We are the light of the world."

Step Two: Learning Acceptance.

I discovered that acceptance is the next step to healing from trauma and tragedy. Accept whatever has happened in your life and recognize what happened truthfully. It was mine and happened to me. Wow, it is easier to say to ourselves, "Why me?" That isn't easy to answer, but it becomes much easier later to look back and see *the why* when life has traveled further. The why usually brings change, a new direction that God felt was needed for our healing.

Aristotle said, *"No matter what the situation, everything happens for a reason, and there is a purpose, meaning, and growth to be gained from whatever tough times you face."*

Accept it as your own and acknowledge that it exists for a purpose. Extract whatever knowledge you can from it. Tragedy significantly deepens our understanding of human nature and fosters compassion and empathy towards others. While we may not be able to physically feel someone else's pain, we can still empathize with them by remembering similar situations and connecting with their emotions. It is crucial to understand that tragedies differ in their severity, and life does not give us a guarantee from them.

It is inherent in human nature to cherish a well-crafted tragedy that concludes with a happy ending in great literature. However, we often cannot predict or anticipate the tragedies that befall us. We can only accept responsibility for what occurs and try to create a good outcome. An essential step is to see whatever needs to be learned from it. Accept it for yourself and others, and then take care of it. You remove the trash from your life when you take care of it (anger, jealousy, hate, or pain). Doggie bag it and let it go! (*But, Please, Don't feed it to your dog.*) I was determined not to let these troubling behaviors continue through me. It is a choice we all have the power to make.

The chaos we create within us is also the chaos outside of us.

What we feel affects everything around us, as in the atmosphere of a serene workplace being changed in seconds. If an angry person walks through a tranquil room, it creates a heavier, darker energy vibrating from their body, affecting everyone else. It is much like the theory of a butterfly in Kansas flapping its wings and creating a slight breeze in London. Everything in the world is interconnected. Every action we take has a ripple effect, causing something else to be influenced elsewhere. Our thoughts and emotions emit energy that resonates and ultimately impacts something or someone else.

Jesus, "Do not be overcome by evil, but overcome evil with good." Romans 12:21

Step Three: Let go of any judgments.

Understanding why people hurt others is impossible, as it is caused by unconscious behavior. I no longer desired to continue adding that constant chatter to our universe. Engaging in an endless stream of thoughts only leads to a never-ending cycle of overthinking that doesn't lead anywhere. You might think that if you have experienced significant pain, why would you want to make others suffer? Unfortunately, hurting someone else creates a feeling of selfish satisfaction for some people. So there, take that!

Put away from you all bitterness, rage, and anger, brawling and slander, together with all malice, and be kind to one another, tenderhearted, and compassionate to one another, forgiving one another, as God in Christ forgave you. Ephesians 4:31

You cannot change others, but wonderfully, you can change any situation by changing yourself.

My early studies taught me that being fearless is necessary for life.

Gandhi said, *"Fearlessness is the first prerequisite of a spiritual life."*

We need not be afraid or concerned about what has not or has already happened, only by looking honestly at everything and knowing that the past is gone and will not return. To move forward, we must embrace fearlessness and acknowledge the existence of the present moment. However, despite this understanding, we often suffer until we reach a breaking point. It may be a life-threatening illness, a major accident, or a tragic event that forces us to delve deeper within ourselves. Only then are we truly willing to accept the profound truths in our lives and release what no longer serves us? This was when my near-death experience interceded in my life to realign me with my true path.

As mindless thoughts spin about,
The pain is its suffering,
It knows no path,
Chaotic and without manner,
Continual agony on an endless track.

Step Four: Surrender and Forgiveness.

The last words told to me in my near-death experience were, "Let It All Go." I needed to surrender everything to God. Surrendering and forgiveness allowed me to open the door to peace and a fresh start toward happiness.

Trust in the Lord with all your heart, and do not rely on your own insight. In all your ways, acknowledge him, and he will make straight your paths.
Proverbs 3:5

I had to put my plans aside and let God's plan unfold. Surrendering and making room for unconditional love means letting go of the ego, which tends to hold us back and prevent us from embracing humility.

Adam and Eve perhaps felt they could be exalted as God themselves and lost the freedom of paradise. Just a little peek at the other side! Our human stuff. We often cannot recognize when we have everything and then gaze over a fence to look for more. How frequently does that get us into trouble? Our pride and ego impede our relationship with God.

Father, if you are willing, remove this cup from me; yet, not my will but yours be done. Luke 22:42

When we surrender everything to the universe, we can see love in everything and everyone as our brother and sister. There is no separation between us or between others, even with nature. We are all connected as brothers and sisters, and our ego gets in the way of enjoying our oneness to everything and everyone. The unconditional love that is the everlasting peace we seek, the moment, the present, the now. It is all there is, and the rest is false.

The future is in the present, while the past is gone.

Forgiving someone is more challenging than simply saying the words. Forgiving someone, or a group of people, from the depths of your soul and heart is a profound experience. It's like your heart is unlocking, allowing the illuminating light of universal consciousness to flow in and replace any emptiness. As we let go and raise our energy while staying grounded in love, we safeguard ourselves from attracting similar personalities in our future journeys.

For if you forgive others their trespasses, your heavenly Father will also forgive you, but if you do not forgive others, neither will your Father forgive your trespasses.
Matthew 6: 14

When we look into the eyes of our faithful cat or dog, we see only their love. Their eyes show no past or future, only the moment. It is easy to love them with all our hearts because we feel their unconditional love. They bring us such a gift. The same is true with a newborn baby's eyes as they have just come from a place of pure love. They arrive in love and depend entirely on us to care for their needs.

So many of us have pets that are such a loving part of our lives, our friends, who love us unconditionally. They are amazing teachers of love.

Be strong and courageous. Do not fear or be in dread of them, for it is
the LORD your God who goes with you. He will not leave you or forsake you."
Deuteronomy 31:6

Our understanding of destructive patterns in our lives brings about necessary change. While other people's problems are not ours, they are ours to overcome if we allow them to affect our lives. I needed to see the lessons in everything and understand their messages. It helps to remember that all this drama in life is not us but the illusions of life. By illusions, I mean things are not always as they seem. Illusions can give us hope, or they can create self-deception. Self-deception, for example, can create the illusion that we do not abuse someone by lying about it whenever asked.

As you keep telling this lie, eventually, you remember only the lie in the future.

But it is still a lie.

But the fruit of the Spirit is love, joy, peace, patience, kindness, goodness, and faithfulness. Galatians 5:22

Carl Gustav Jung said, *"The difference between a good life and a bad life is how well you walk through the fire."*

Perhaps further explanation is needed, as walking through it well will also mean you learn to heal and let it all go as you walk.

When life spirals downward, the situation will often require a life-changing event to put us back on the path we have strayed from. The event can come in many forms and can be a significant life-threatening disease or, in my case, a near-death experience. We often meet people in life who claim cancer, or some disease was the best thing that happened to them, because it forced them to change their lives in a good way.

When God began to create heaven and earth–the earth being unformed and void, with darkness over the surface of the deep and a wind from God sweeping over the water …. Genesis 1:1

Have you ever considered the fire which
you kindle?
Is it you who have brought into being the
tree
Which feeds the fire, or is it We Who cause
it to grow?
It is We Who have made it a reminder,
And a comfort for those who wander in the
wilderness,
Then celebrate the limitless glory
of the Name of your Sustainer, the Most
High.

—Sürah Al-Wâq

Nothing can harm you as much as your own thoughts unguarded." Buddha

Chapter Four

A World of Prayer

A World of Prayer

At birth, we take our first breath of life to begin life and animate our body, and later, our final breath of life is at the end of our journey when we become still.

Whatsoever you ask in my name, this I will do, that the Father may be glorified in the son. John 14:13

I was walking on and preferring to think beyond tough times, recognizing them as only steps in our life path, momentary hurdles to step over. Still, I feel astounded at how it all works so rightly. As I continued my walk, the woods seemed vibrant this morning. The birds appeared lively, singing and chirping, while the bushy-tailed squirrels rustled through the leaves and scurried far up in the trees as messengers of our glorious universe. I walked along in the brisk air, remembering my similar childhood walks through the seed-studded cones of the great pine trees in their final fall days. Soon, the cones would fall to the ground. I would gather a few to place in my secret box of admired treasures. It was opened only on special occasions to marvel at and enjoy the citrusy pine fragrances and intricate layers of conifer scales. Among the pines were tall white birches mingled with heart-shaped leaves and the beauty of peeling bark. As children, we used the peels to shape into perfect bark canoes to sail on the flow of the river stream. None could imagine our delight in watching them bobbing along the stream while we stood on the muddy banks with our pant legs rolled high, shoes off, and toes squishing in the mud, all in unrestrained joy and enthusiasm.

Reading the words of Rabbi Nachman of Breslav, the late-eighteenth-century sage, captured my soul with...

"How good is it to pray to God and meditate in the meadows and fields amidst the grass and trees. When one goes out to the meadows to pray, every blade of grass, every plant and flower enters his prayers and helps him, putting strength and force into his words."

So many memories and learnings carried me through life as reverence for all of nature and the finding of our divinity through the frolicking of children with no less fervor than Tom Sawyer or Huck Finn themselves. Nature opens our imagination with such illumination that we must stand in awe.

Nothing is without voice: God everywhere can hear Arising from creation His praise and echo clear.

You travel far and wide To scout and see and search;
If God you fail to see, You have nothing observed.
-Angelus Silesius

I remember that day well when I first chose to release everything into the hands of the universe and *let it all go*.

It wasthe final necessary step to my healing. It was a fall day, and I had just picked flowers from last summer to fill my favorite vase for the table. The sweet-scented flowers' fragrance captured the room. I poured myself some tea and sat comfortably in a favorite stuffed chair. I could feel the calmness of my whole body as a quiet peace spread through me.

I blessed each cell of my body while a calm presence and stillness encapsulated my entire being as *"a peace that passes all understanding."* I could feel the aliveness in my hands and continue through my body. I acknowledged my pain and asked the universe to absorb it from my heart and release me from fear. I prayed for a transformation of any darkness into pure white light. I intended to *let it all go* and allow divine love to *take charge* of my life and guide me. When we genuinely forgive, we enjoy peace of mind that blesses us with the true happiness of life. If thoughts of our story and pain continue, we must continue our work diligently.

It can take years for so much pain to build up in us and then years to release it. We must always be diligent as healing continues throughout life and is a constant process.

Praying creates our perfect reunion with our universe's super consciousness or light force. Prayers must come from the deepest part of our hearts to surpass the darkness. Our oneness must travel from the mind to the heart, where our prayer must be felt, and we must know that everything has already been accomplished.

Spread your wings and pray from your heart. Feel it and be the light!

"God passes through the thicket of the world, and wherever his glance falls he turns all things to beauty." –Saint John of the Cross

When I begin my prayers, it is like striking a match. When I say Dear God, the flame bursts alive, creating light and warmth. My words are the action as I begin my conversation with the universe, allowing the words to flow effortlessly and with concentration from the heart. My words are my communication with the universe; feeling the words is how we send our prayers by speaking from the heart to reveal our love, needs, and desires. To start, take a few deep breaths and gently place your hand over your heart. As you do this, allow your breathing to slow down. Direct your focus towards your words and sincerely connect with the emotions and intentions they carry. Through prayer, you can establish a profound connection with the universe, confident that your prayers have already been fulfilled. Through feeling, your prayer moves from the mind to the heart. This is where your healing takes place. It is where we connect and are anointed with the spark of divine Love. Like picking up our phone and quietly saying, "Hello."

The light and our angels are there to listen. At the close of my prayer, I acknowledge God's love and accept God's gifts in my life with gratitude. I allow myself to go deeper into the silence, breathing and knowing the words spoken are now in the universal consciousness of love.

There is no memory of the words that left my heart to become part of the universal consciousness. They are no longer mine, as they belong to the collective consciousness. Our voice is the energy, while our lips shape the words that create our method of communication. It is powerful as everything spoken creates energy carried out into our universe.

After prayer, I allow myself to unwind and immerse myself in the serene embrace of divine love. I cherish the moments of divine awareness and true peace that follow my prayers. Sometimes, I let my mind wander and conjure the enchanting image of lotus blossoms and candles drifting down the river Ganges. I appreciate how the power of imagination allows us to journey anywhere and almost feel the energy of another mystical place. Through the power of my mind, I can visualize the magnificent sight of floating lamps made with candles and beautiful lotus blossoms.

It is a lovely vision of them being set free at dusk on the river Ganges while floating along in perfect unison along the riverbank. Guided down the river by the Goddess Ma Ganga, the blossoms and candles represent a physical prayer. I imagine seeing my prayer floating along as a Lotus blossom (called diyas), dancing in the glow of all the other lighted candles with prayers to be heard by the ones who hear our prayers. It is such a glorious vision that I can almost feel the chanting and singing while the sitar and bamboo flutes play along with all those celebrating. It is an enchanting and memorable way to end my prayers.

God hears every prayer. Our words carry our energy to the ears of God, as our breath communicates with God's vibration of the universe. When we allow ourselves to vibrate, as the master Schneur Zaiman describes with

"The Breath of his mouth," it will feel like the very wind itself as all things in life and the universe vibrate with the *Breathe of his mouth.*

Our Father in heaven
Hallowed be your name.
Your Kingdom come,
Your will be done,
On earth as it is in heaven.
Give us this day our daily bread,
And forgive us our debts,
As we also have forgiven our debtors,
And "lead us not into temptation,
but deliver us from evil." Matthew 6:10

Since early childhood, I have loved watching the motion of the ocean. Nothing is more soothing than listening to and watching God breathe through nature. I would stand on the shores to hear the breath drawing in and then the exhalation of letting out with the constant undulation of each wave pushing into shore. The in and out of God's breath aligns me with the universe, peace, and serenity. The prayers in this book can guide you so you can write your own or enjoy interpreting mine in your own words. Prayers have continued to be the most essential part of my life.

When God began to create heaven and earth–the earth being unformed and void, with darkness over the surface of the deep and a wind from God sweeping over the water ….

Gregg Braden speaks so illustriously about Prayer through our heart and how it tells a language to our body created each time our heart beats. The neurons respond to our feelings and can harmonize the heart and brain. It is a powerful energy at 0.1 Hz connecting our words, emotions, and feelings sent as our message into the universe.

It is suggested that we take three minutes daily to focus on slowing our breathing—a time to allow breathing to be slower than normal. Then, breathe slowly in and out while keeping your focus and awareness on your heart. Placing your hand over the heart helps to keep the focus there. This will harmonize the heart and brain and strengthen your immune system by eliminating all the day's stresses.

It is a powerful way to keep the body at its best.

0.1Hz = Love!

Science has learned what the ancients, mystics, and Yogis have always known. True healing comes when the heart and brain harmonize. When we touch our hearts and slow our breathing, the body relaxes and feels safe. This sends a calming chemistry to the body, where we can feel the emotions of gratitude and gratefulness. The heart allows us to move out of the polarity of right and wrong. It moves us to a place that will enable the heart's intelligence to observe, honor, and let things go by shifting the mind into the heart. It puts us in a space I remember feeling beyond the veil. It opens the neurons to allow the energy to flow freely and metabolize out of the body the unhealthy chemicals of our pain and trauma—the unresolved issues within us.

Jesus said, "Bring forth that which is within you, and it will save you. Deny that which is within you, and it will destroy you." This means that denying the love within us will destroy us.

Rainer Maria Rilke writes in The Book of Hours that God "*walks with us silently out of the night.*" *As we move closer to where the light is coming in, God whispers,*

Let everything happen to you: beauty and terror.
Just keep going....
Don't let yourself lose me.

We have all shared those moments when taking another step seems too much. I have been there and remember praying for God not to let go of my hand in those moments. Thankfully, God never let go.

The Lord is close to the brokenhearted and saves those who are crushed in spirit.

Psalm 34:18

If prayer is pure and untainted,
surely that holy breath
that rises from your lips
Will join with the breath of heaven
that is always flowing
into you from above.........
Thus that part of God
Which is within you
Is reunited with its source.
—Hasi

The wolf shall dwell with the lamb, And
the leopard shall lie down with the kid...
Isaiah 11:6

Chapter Five

Feeling Apart From Everyone

Feeling Apart From Everyone

I Feel Lonely.

Somedays, I feel so lonely.
Then, I remembered that I was never alone.
Love is all around me.
It appears in so many ways. The smile of a
parent or friend. A kitten rubbing against my
leg. I watched a bird singing on my
windowsill.
The daffodils blowing in the wind. The sun
glistened on my porch. A friend's voice on
my phone.
Love is everywhere, and everywhere is you.
Forgive my forgetfulness. I am your grateful
child.
Thank you.
Amen

When we grow up and choose our path in
life, we begin to wake up to a new

reality, and it can be lonely if we choose a spiritual path. As children, we are not taught the core life skills to build the foundation of a happy future. School curriculums do not teach us the things needed for a spiritual path, as we will need to develop those skills independently when we learn the requirements of living self-reliantly.

Awakening becomes our path to discovering who we are, our truth. As we awaken, we are no longer driven by what our parents, relatives, teachers, or society tell us. We are waking up to a higher reality.

We recognize that our life no longer requires a fancy car or many admiring friends. While nice things and friends are fantastic, we start to place more value on the things less critical to life and happiness, our inner peace of mind.

Turn to me and be gracious to me, for I am lonely and afflicted. Relieve the troubles of my heart and bring me out of my distress. Psalms 25:16

Jesus knew loneliness but then said, "I *am not alone, for my Father is with me."* John 16:32

Jesus knew what it was to be comforted even in the face of abandonment. When loneliness feels overwhelming, we must first turn our attention from what we lack to what we do have.

Feelings don't always come with an explanation; they can exist as a sense of being lost or overwhelmed. It can be feelings of the loss of someone we loved. There is confusion about why they die. It can be feelings remembered when seeing something that brings a memory of sadness to mind. A specific food, smell, or even a piece of music reminds us of someone or something locked away in our hearts. We can find ourselves suddenly sobbing with feelings of loneliness or grief. It's normal to have these feelings, so we should acknowledge them by feeling and embracing them, then releasing them through self-love and pampering. Take all the time required to move through the process until you feel ready to step forward in life again. Be at peace.

This short daily practice can help. Focus on your heart in the center of your chest for a few minutes daily. Breathe in and out, very relaxed and natural, while keeping your attention there. Allow any feelings or sensations to arise and pass slowly away. If your attention drifts away, gently focus to bring it back to your heart. After a few minutes, open your eyes and take the time to notice the centeredness. Doing this daily will help you to feel the difference between being centered and being distracted by the ego. As we grow in our understanding of the abundance within us, which is nurtured through daily prayer and meditation, our longing for external validation, which often leads to loneliness and dependence on others or material possessions, will gradually dissipate.

Remember that loneliness doesn't solely result from lacking people in our lives. Instead, it originates from a feeling of inner emptiness. Let's embrace others as they are, acknowledging that we are all distinct individuals. We are journeying together toward a better destination, but we are progressing at our own pace and uniquely. Let's remember that it is ultimately our own choices and free will that shape our path.

While I do not follow any religion, I take

the pieces that feel true to me and let go of anything that does not. Each religion has its way of messaging, but all are gloriously about love. Love is our connection to God; it can be God, Buddha, Mohammed, Jesus, or the universal consciousness, or, as some call it, the Light force.

Every one of us possesses a universal connection to something greater, propelling us to reach new heights. This connection serves as a guiding force, leading us towards profound aspirations for the betterment of our souls. Jesus may have chosen a path that the world was not yet ready for, and perhaps it remains unprepared to comprehend fully. However, before departing from this familiar world, he entrusted his teachings to his devoted disciples and scribes, ensuring that his wisdom would endure. While changed here and there in bits and pieces, the message of Love has survived two thousand years or more and has the same teachings as all the other Masters. It is a story of Love.

It is about realizing our connection, loving one another, and fulfilling our life path.

I pray we are getting closer to achieving this self-awareness that will bring about the peaceful world we all yearn for and envision.

God is the friend of silence.
See how nature–trees, flowers, grass–
grows in silence; see the stars, the moon,
and the sun, how they move in silence.
We need silence to be able to touch souls.
–Mother Theresa

Finding the infinite joy of the spirit within you and the connection to something far more significant than ourselves is when we realize we are total oneness with the universe and never alone.

Peaceful Sleep

As I lie down each night, may it be in peace.
May my nights be only of tranquil sleep.
Sleeping free of any disturbing thoughts or dreams.
Allowing me to awaken refreshed each glorious morning.
To go about my day feeling only peace.
Grateful for your love and guiding presence.

Seeing me safely along my way. Amen

How can you buy or sell the sky, the warmth of the land? If we do not own the freshness of the air and the sparkle of the water, how can you buy them?
—Suquamish Chief

Chapter Six
Becoming New

Becoming New

It's fall, and the leaves have created a carpet of colors everywhere. Today, while strolling in my yard and walking through a vibrant carpet of leaves, I stopped to find the mended branch from years earlier. The end of the branch had been nearly severed, leaving it barely attached and receiving just enough nutrients to continue to survive.

A brave and daring branch hanging on for life when a whipping wind could easily dismember the flaying piece. Using florist tape and string, I created a makeshift splint.

Two years later, the lilac branch is fully healed and bloomed this past spring, spreading a delightful fragrance throughout the yard. Even without my attempts to assist the branch, it endeavored to recover using its innate intelligence to repair itself while barely able to hang on. Nature reveals this incredible healing aptitude that we also share.

While studying the branch, I was reminded of a lady who had lost part of her hand in an accident. Months later, while looking out her dining-room window, she noticed a new limb replacing a lost one on a tree in her backyard.

She wondered if the tree could do that, then why couldn't she? After all, are we not a part of nature, like the tree?

In the following years since I started my healing process, I have dwelled within the depths of my being, engaging in meditation and prayer. I discover that I am in a perpetual state of transformation, experiencing those enlightening "Ahaa" moments when fresh understanding dawns upon me. I understand and remember how the memories of pain linger. Moving painful memories from our brains (the brain is a polarity organ that recognizes things as right or wrong) to our hearts (that is not a polarity organ) by meditation requires time, practice, and determination. Doing so enables us to process these memories objectively in the heart without guilt or judgment. This releases the blockages in our bodies and grants us freedom and healing.

Healing from Trauma is not an easy process as our body suffers a great shock and creates many impulses that move through every cell of our being: fear. Muscles tighten, the heart beats faster with shallow breathing from lack of oxygen; we feel cold and clammy, and brain waves are affected as we go into a different state of awareness, fright, fight, and even emotional numbness we are changed at a cellular level.

Our body's cells contain the chemical equivalent of every experience. The emotional changes created by trauma are then anchored in the organs and tissues of our body. The tightening of the cells and neurons blocks the flow of energy, and the cells and organs of our body are stuck in that moment of trauma.

What happened with my mom was so powerful that throughout my early childhood, I had no conscious memory of anything; everything remained tucked away in my subconscious. I suppose it was my way of self-protection. It wasn't until high school and later that I started having flashbacks of something I had always subconsciously known had happened. Being a child, it was truly overwhelming, mainly because I still lived with the person who caused the pain. Consequently, I chose to bury those memories deep within my subconscious until later, when I could handle the memory of what had happened.

Trauma has a devastating impact on society as the suffering experienced by children affected by war or violence can be imprinted in their DNA for up to three generations. The body's cellular memory, encoded in DNA, is believed to retain these traumatic experiences. Now, we know that it is retained not only in our cells but also in our brains and hearts' memory.

This is the legacy we pass onto our young women through society's violence in the DNA of future mothers. We currently lack knowledge of how this impacts their children, as studies are still incomplete. However, it is known that the effects can remain for three or even more generations. The persistent cycle of pain resulting from violence, rape, and terror, deeply ingrained in our society, continues to be passed down from one generation to the next.

People do not need to be of any religion or faith to know that something greater than themselves is within them. Breathe and believe in your heart the goodness of God and the life meant for you and everyone.

Without our inner connection to something

greater, we might rely on addictions, violence, and other social problems to fill that empty place within. When we forget our connections with others and the universe, we are isolated, lost in a vast world, and wonder about its meaning. Where there is a void, something will rush in to fill it. It is up to us what we want to fill that void with and to be like a newborn child. To see everything fresh, as in a child's innocence that is so precious as the world has not yet fashioned them, they see everything in its purity and freshness. When children see another child with skin a different color, there is no fear, as they only see a new chum and run-off playing together.

Children lose their innocence when they learn fears and prejudices from their elders and society. Adults accumulate a wealth of experiences, knowledge, and perspectives throughout their lives. These experiences shape their filters, which can be either beneficial or detrimental. Certain filters can significantly damage their physical well-being, necessitating immense determination and strength to recover.

As adults, we must take responsibility for

ourselves and our lives. We can reach out to the incredible source that lies within our hearts, a source that can heal our every need. Once we've mastered the four steps to healing and meditation, we can easily discern what feels true to us and bring more profound healing and meaning into our lives. Soul healing is like standing on a peaceful shoreline, where the gentle breeze whispers through the tall grass, and the soft sound of waves crashing against the shore fills the air. It's about closing our eyes and inhaling the scent of the salty sea as our inner voice gently nudges us toward our true passions and desires.

My favorite thing to do is kneading bread. The kneading process does not need thought, as the hands know exactly what to do. The mind can feel peace and a serene connection with everything around me, even the world. It's a special connection that softens the day and reconnects me with my divine source, the universe, or God. It is also yours, and how you communicate with God is yours.

No religion is needed, but only the heart to connect with what we feel is faithful to us. Listen to your inner voice, have unwavering belief, and shape the reality that aligns with your aspirations.

Sometimes, I experience a deep sense of peace that engulfs my entire being. These moments of serene silence bring me solace as I indulge in the captivating sights and sounds around me or lose myself in the pages of an inspiring book. The breathtaking beauty of scenic places mesmerizes me, allowing me to contemplate any worries that burden my mind while I patiently await their resolution.

At times, the answer reveals itself to me instantly, while other times, it takes a bit longer to materialize. During my meditation sessions, I prioritize taking slow, deep breaths, directing my attention to my heart and breath. This practice enables me to reach a state of profound relaxation, fully embracing the calmness and serenity of the present moment as I inhale the peacefulness surrounding me. As I breathe in, I embrace the peacefulness that envelops me, transitioning from the mind to the realm of the heart. In this place, our healing occurs, and our connection to the universe is nurtured.

Afterward, I am always left with a sense of rejuvenation, centeredness, and serenity. It reminds us that the universe shines brighter when we connect with our divine consciousness and know our voices are already heard and acknowledged.

"Peace be with you!" Then Yeshua told Thomas, "Put your finger here; see my hands. Reach out your hand and put it into my side. Stop doubting and believe."

–From The Gospels of Thomas.

Chapter Seven

Alone with God

Aristotle said, "Give me seven years of a child's life, and I will show you the man."

Alone with God

"Hello World, how are you today?" I think I started saying this each morning as a child. Then, I would review what I wanted to accomplish in my day. My day planner!

As a child, it was simple little things like finding a spot to build a hut of branches in the woods and later planning what was necessary for life, family, and work. The size of things changed, but their importance was only relative to my years. I firmly believe we are the creators of our lives and can create everything we desire through our beliefs, thoughts, and actions.

What we contribute to the world will return to us through friendships, accomplishments, a fulfilling marriage, a meaningful life, and overall happiness. I refused to let all the pain of so many years define me. There is so much beauty in the world and so much joy to experience. When we have the unfortunate experience of having a family that doesn't support us or people who seem to feel as though they are extinguishing our very existence, this could be a persistent karmic issue that has followed us from past lives or a current situation in our present life. Acknowledging this and transitioning to a better place is the key to our healing and progress. It is time to embrace healing, allowing ourselves to move forward and release the pain that never reflected our true selves. We are all beings of love, and we are all deeply loved.

That was my story a few decades ago before taking my first steps to change my life. I had determined not to spend the rest of my life suffering. Throughout my early life, I suffered from thoughts and ideas that had nothing to do with my creation. I had allowed the problems of others to hinder me from the joy and flowering of life, the happiness we all deserve. Healing is a magical and incredible journey, as each day presents new opportunities for change and growth. Today, we experience the most amazing opportunities as science continues to open new doors to understanding our body and its power. The science of DNA has brought many advancements in the study of our bodies, aided by the knowledge our ancients already knew and practiced. Now, we are privileged to see how science can beautifully merge with the spiritual understanding of our past, allowing us to

109

move forward boldly in greater wisdom. A world of peace awaits us if we harness technology responsibly and never forget the divine nature of our bodies and existence. My work has brought me the healing and peace of mind I had longed for. I am sharing my journey in the hopes that it may help you. However, always trust your inner guidance and seek medical assistance when needed.

In my early thirties, I embarked on a healing journey. And as I approached retirement, yes, the delightful golden age finally greeted me! During this time, I decided to compile a list of my ten personal goals. I meditate daily on these goals, visualizing and experiencing each step as if they were already achieved. This exercise has proven to be incredibly powerful for me. Not only does my list of goals continually evolve, allowing space for new aspirations, but it also harnesses the power of my mind and heart to create positive changes in my DNA. To let go of any old, stubborn remaining patterns. The harmonious communication between our brain and heart holds incredible power, capable of influencing the cells within our body. This allows light into areas once hindered by darkness and tension so our bodies can fully express the essence of love. Science can now show how our body interacts with the brain and heart. What a fantastic time we live in, but also potentially dangerous if we misuse our technology to sidestep our divinity. The mesmerizing symphony of our brain and heart harmonizing, like a delicate ballet, can paint a vivid picture of the world and nurture the temple of our healthy body. As we allow the pulsating rhythm of our heartbeat to create an intricate neural pathway, every possibility will linger in the air. With each heartbeat aligned with our intentions, we have the power to shape any reality we yearn for. And I believe we all yearn for peace and happiness for ourselves and the world. The flowering of our planet is to live in kindness and friendship with each other as brothers and sisters. A place where we can walk freely in safety to enjoy the planet's harmony and balance of nature in our lives. We live on a beautiful planet with oceans, lakes, streams, and land covered with the growth of nature while surrounded by trees to meet the needs of our environment and bodies. We are incredibly fortunate to witness the beauty surrounding us, from the vibrant hues of blooming flowers to the majestic sight of towering mountains. It is our solemn responsibility to safeguard this precious gift, not just for our own sake but also for the survival of our planet itself. The wonderful earthy scent of fresh rain and the soft touch of a gentle

111

breeze remind us of the delicate balance we must preserve.

Years ago, with a friend on a dazzling, usual Hawaiian sunny day on Makiki Street, we were headed to our favorite ice cream shop with just enough money to buy our famous coffee ice cream cones when I commented that all we needed to complete the day was the Sunday paper to read while enjoying our ice cream. Suddenly, the beautiful Hawaii trade winds swept across all the patios nearby, sending twirling pages around us in the air and landing perfectly at our feet. The Sunday paper was all completely folded neatly. Bending over and picking it up, I commented, "Ask, and you shall receive!" while my friend said, "No, this is not asked, and you shall receive. This is *Scary*! Every time I get near you, the strangest things happen." I replied that when you and God and your faith are all alone in the world, strange things do happen. My uncertain but accepting friend finally smiled as we walked on to buy our ice cream cones and enjoy our Sunday paper—new beginnings.

Through my various experiences, I have

gained a deep understanding of the hardships that others endure and have learned to cherish the inner beauty that resides within their hearts. However, I also recognize the importance of safeguarding ourselves by remaining mindful of people's true nature and potential actions. My ability to empathize with their pain, which reflects my own, allows me to feel compassion for them.

Like a fleeting whisper, the past fades from our grasp, yet its imprint on our character and uniqueness remains. But it lacks the authority to define us. Our essence, a radiant reflection deep within, surpasses the bounds of life's encounters. In the ancient Gnostic gospels, Jesus stressed the significance of rekindling our innate nature - the very essence of our humanity that resides within our hearts - *love.*

Chapter Eight

How Life Blends

How Life Blends

As an amateur writer, I have devoted countless hours to crafting this book and coming to terms with my trauma and hurts. I humbly ask for your forgiveness for any imperfections or inadequacies that may have slipped into my writing. I have shared what little I have learned and experienced. I remain a student of learning and know there is still so much more to learn. Each day seems to unveil fresh revelations.

I have learned that life here on earth can be difficult and requires much patience, love, kindness, and prayer. At times, we may feel like we are desperately clinging to the side of a boat as the ocean waves toss us around. But when we feel hopeless, a helicopter suddenly appears to rescue us. Sometimes, that "helicopter" is nothing more than faith itself. The faith that no matter what is happening, *this too will pass*. Everything eventually passes. We have all experienced this many times when we feel we cannot hold on for another moment, but somehow, we manage to. Help always arrived, even if it wasn't in the form expected, and sometimes, and usually most often at the very last second!

I was very fortunate that throughout my childhood, my parents and I went on wonderful trips in the Maine woods, to the Ogunquit Playhouse, or by ferry to the islands around the Maine coast. Mom and I canned over two hundred quarts of vegetables each year for our winter food. We had beautiful Christmases, and in high school, my parents saw that I had everything I needed.

Even though, as a child, I was aware of the existence of love and caring, I couldn't feel it in my heart. Material possessions could never replace the absence of affectionate touches, comforting words, and warm hugs. What I felt was always the proverbial elephant in the room, silently yearning for answers that never arrived. It took years of healing to discover the confidence and self-worth needed to demand what was rightfully mine from life: *love*. Until that realization, my emotions remained locked away, and I patiently waited to discover the key that would set me free.

Although many positive experiences occurred during my childhood, I always felt that void regarding receiving love and feeling wanted. I didn't feel unique or beautiful. My emotional state seemed repressed to the point that I couldn't even shed tears when feeling sad.

I vividly remember an incident years ago when I was riding a bus in Honolulu and saw two lovely young ladies sitting across from me. They were dressed in charming feminine dresses, eyes sparkling as they bubbled with happiness, talking with one another. I was enchanted and tried to determine why they drew my attention so much. Then I realized that behind these gentle-mannered and soft-speaking delightful young women were two beautiful, loving mothers. These lovely young women had been mothered and were a delicious reflection of that motherly love. I felt joy for them. I don't know if my mother had experienced that with her mother, but I do know how it feels when it is missing—the power of a hug, kiss, and touch that makes us feel wanted and loved.

Sometimes, we are not loved or feel loved by people who should love us. Then we learn it is not about us, that a child has done nothing wrong when love, affection, and caring are not returned. It is about the parent being dismissive or unable to show that affection. Once you realize it is their unhealed emotional fragility, it is easy to forgive and even feel compassion. Their behavior isn't right or wrong; it is just what it is: an unhealed fragility that projects a painful lack onto someone else.

Luckily, as adults, if a situation continues to be too painful, we can distance ourselves from the person or situation. There's no need for regrets; it's all part of life and the learning process. I've traveled a long, winding road filled with various experiences that have led me to this moment of happiness. Once we've moved past our childhood, it's not someone else's responsibility to make us happy. Instead, it's up to us to fill our hearts and allow them to overflow with joy. We should discover what brings us happiness and pursue it abundantly. Perhaps only then can we truly experience the joy of sharing with others.

To See God everywhere is to see Oneself in everything.

Our hundred-acre wood, where I was privileged to spend my youth taught me the importance of nature in our lives. It was the music of my soul. My days in our hundred-acre wood became my Thoreauvian experience, which is why Walden profoundly touched me. Thoreau got from becoming one with nature, which is what others got from sitting in church. It was his holies of holies, where the trees were his cathedral.

His sense of the divine has spoken to me throughout my life. Whenever I feel lost or alone, I think of his words and him as a kindred soul who could talk to my differentness.

Live in each season as it passes; breathe the air, drink the drink, taste the fruit, and resign yourself to the influences of each. Let them be your only diet drink and botanical medicines. –Henry David Thoreau

We will encounter numerous scenarios throughout our lives. I am fortunate to have immersed my childhood in nature, which allowed me to truly grasp the profound connection between spirituality and the natural world. God understands that we are bound to make mistakes or choose incorrectly, but our purpose is to gain knowledge from these experiences. It would be simpler if we could be flawless and avoid errors, but unfortunately, we are only human.

Life will bring us various scenarios as we journey through it. It might seem more convenient if we could all reside in desert tents like the Egyptian Desert Fathers, where interactions with other humans are minimal or nonexistent. However, what other challenges could arise while living alone in the desert apart from dealing with the bothersome animal bug kingdom? But since most of us have families, jobs, neighbors, children, etc., we interact with the human world and have opportunities for all sorts of blessings, family, and mishaps.

My teachers in the ministry often refer to mistakes as errors in thinking, which opens up the possibility for correction. I believe that God feels the same way. Each day presents us with a new chance for these possibilities. Through discipline, we are given a fresh start to strive for greater heights and achieve new goals. It's truly amazing to realize that our passions hold endless possibilities. By joining hands with our fellow brothers and sisters, we have the power to create a planet filled with love and peaceful souls simply by loving one another.

It took me a large part of my lifetime to learn that it is through tragedies that we gain a greater sense of purpose. The glory of God is within us when we do. I seemed to view my sufferings early in life as just my lot in

life until later, during healing, I learned to embrace my tragedies as not my lot in life, or anyone's, but the opportunity to rise above difficult circumstances, afflictions, and sufferings to find greater strength with God. No one understood this better than St. Paul in his beautiful letters to the Philippians, called the Epistle of Joy in the eleventh book of the New Testament.

As my parents have departed to join God, I pray for their new journey. Throughout our lives, we shared, grew, learned, and enjoyed each other's company, embracing whatever roles we had. Their journey will continue beyond this world as learning and personal growth are everlasting. We are promised eternal life, ensuring that our journey remains endless. Later, during healing, I learned to embrace my tragedies as not my lot in life, or anyone's, but the opportunity to rise above difficult circumstances, afflictions, and sufferings to find greater strength with God.

My parents and I embarked on a journey together, albeit not flawlessly, that I believe brought growth to us all. I am thankful for the days and years we shared and for how every experience helped shape the person I am today. I express my gratitude for that.

Dear God, *Thank you for my parents and our shared journey. I pray for their eternal rest, peace, and love as they pursue God's next plan. I pray that my mom has peace and love for her wholeness. I know God is blessing and helping her. May we always love and bless each other, and may my parents know my gratitude for giving me life. I pray we let go of any pain or sorrow and feel and embrace only your love. I Believe, and so it is, Amen.*

Jesus promised, I give unto them eternal life; and they shall never perish. –John 10:27

I slowly began to unwind my steps back home and the thought of the warm waiting fireplace, my favorite chair, and home. Home is where the heart resides, along with my dearest loving husband and darling kitty, Edwin Hubble. Edwin is an elegant tuxedo kitty that came to us through Tara Rescue Service that brought us this perfectly well-mannered bucket of love. My loving and kind husband and I have shared over thirty incredible years. We are a family while our siblings and children live in Hawaii and are spread across the country. So many blessings! Technology keeps us and our friends connected and informed about everyone's daily life. As I approach the path to our front door, my walk takes on a new skip as I am happy to be home and invigorated by such a pleasant walk-in nature. The fireplace will quickly take away the day's chill. Everything in my life has allowed me to see God's beautiful goodness. The most minor things give us the greatest joyfulness: a touch, a smile, a breeze blowing on our face, the sun's warmth, all these gifts of Goodness. A loving shoulder to lay my head on while sharing movies. The intoxicating smile of a loved one. The joy of each stunning season as we plant our flowers together and enjoy watching everything grow. The peace of sitting together on the porch, listening to the rippling sound of fountain water while birds overhead sing melodies of song in trees and branches. The pleasantry of warm cocoa shared when sitting near the fire in winter; all this and so much more are gifted to us as God's goodness. These moments fill our hearts and touch our souls to become cherished memories to treasure. Our greatest blessings are the bliss of love from family, friends, neighbors, coworkers and all the kindnesses we can share throughout each day. While this physical show of love was missing during my childhood, it came in abundance later in life. Our eyes suddenly open when healed to attract and appreciate our lives filled with Goodness. God's goodness is all free to receive.

We are the writers of our book of life; we are its author who writes every word and deed through what we say and do.

If your mind becomes firm like a rock and no longer shakes
In a world where everything is shaking, Your mind will be your greatest friend. And suffering will not come your way.
                          –Buddha

Glimmers of hope emerge when we perceive the world through a brighter lens, where colors are more vibrant, laughter echoes in the air, and the sweet scent of optimism fills our nostrils.

"*You never enjoy the world aright, till the sea itself floweth in your veins, till you are clothed with the heavens, and crowned with the stars; and perceive yourself to be the sole heir of the whole world and more . . . because men are in it who are every one of them sole heirs as well as you. . . Till your spirit fills the whole world, and the stars are your jewels.*"
– Thomas Traherne

I have been incredibly honored to share the vibrant tapestry of my life with you, the readers of my book. Your graciousness in inviting me into your world and embracing my story fills my heart with deep gratitude. May my family's journey and experiences resonate within you, serving as guiding lights along your path. As you delve into this chronicle, you may discover words that touch your soul, fulfilling any longing.

May the words within these pages ignite a fire within you, like a crackling bonfire on a starlit night, illuminating the depths of your soul. May they fulfill any longing, like the comforting scent of freshly baked cookies, wrapping you in a warm embrace on a cold winter's night. My heart overflows with gratitude, knowing that my words have found a home within your hearts, resonating like a harmonious melody that lingers. Science has opened new doors for us. We now have the opportunity to blend ancient knowledge with modern science. And there will be more to come. It is truly a glorious time to be alive.

May all your days be filled with the warmest Love, wrapping you in its comforting embrace, and many Hugs to bring joy and warmth to your heart!

Part Two

Sophie's Letters

Letters To Sophie

After arriving home and grabbing a quick shower to remove the morning's beaded heat, I settled into my favorite soft chair to begin writing the message I heard from the soul of nature witnessed that morning and from my heart.

As I began, I needed to align my thinking with the words of God.

Dear God, your precious child, Sophie, was cruelly attacked. I am praying that you will use me to help Sophie and her family. May my written words and thoughts be your words and thoughts, and may your love and light lift her above all that has happened. I pray for Sophie to continue being the confident, loving, caring, beautiful soul you created her to be.

I pray for Sophie to rise above the evil, pain, and drama of a misguided and lost soul. While Justice is yours, I trust you will deal with this perfectly in fairness. I pray for Sophie's soul to be free and able to forgive the person who caused this terrible harm.

I pray this in the name and Love of Jesus Christ, our Savior. Thank you. Amen.

I moved to my desk and pulled out a sheet of paper. I decided to use one with a delicate ripple engraved through it. And began to write:

Dearest Darling Sophie,

Thank you for contacting me and sharing your pain. I am saddened and sorry for what you have suffered. I am honored to try and share anything I can to help. You have asked how I endured similar pain. Words seem to fall short of expressing such difficult things, but I will try my very best to tell you what I can.

I was told of the dreadful tragedy that befell your life, and it is always complex to understand the cruelty of others. It must be terrible for someone not to feel God. I think people who do such horrible things are in that awful space, feeling all alone. Sadly, there are people in so much pain that they want someone else to suffer and feel their pain, too. For what might only be a brief moment, their pain is so great that we could only say they reacted as an unconscious person in insanity or madness. During those horrific, cruel moments, they lose control and are themselves being controlled by evil or certainly not by their better angels.

We are reminded of this when we remember Jesus speaking to his Father from the cross and saying, "Father, forgive them, for they know not what they do."

Sometimes, understanding a person can help us forgive, but it does not mean we can forget or that understanding will lessen our pain. It will help, but the pain is real. You will face many challenges in the coming years, but I know you will meet them with great resolve and be strengthened by everything. I can feel your strength in your letter. Your strength will carry you through all this to a place of peace and a good life—the beautiful life God planned for you. God knows your dreams, every one of them, and those are also his dreams for you.

I want you always to know that while I am not there with you in person, I am here, joined with you in heart, prayers, and spirit. Until our letters meet again, I know you will be strong in faith and spirit, remembering God is with you, as my constant caring and prayers are always with you.

I am blowing you a sky full of kisses of love. Can you Catch them?

I am seeing you Wrapped in the warmest blessings of love.

Mary-Eisa.

As I addressed the envelope and placed it in it, I grappled with the dreadfulness of the moment. Sophie is so young and suffered so much. It will take great strength, courage, and all the support we can give her to survive her ordeal. She will soon ask the most difficult question: Why and where was God when a horrible person attacked such a beautiful young woman and badly cut her face in a last moment of vileness to deprive her of her beauty and maidenhood of innocence? May God's love and wisdom be with me. God, please have your hand on this. Please help me, help her, with you. I know her pain, and still, I struggle with how some do such terrible things. Sophie's attacker was unknown to her but had left her emotionally imprinted for life. Life contains many unanswerable questions about our fellow man.

*Justice is not ours to do
but the work of God.*

These are all tremendous situations to wrestle with, and we go deeply within ourselves to find the place within our hearts to love no matter what happens to us.

> *I said in my heart, God will judge the*
> *righteous and the wicked, for he has*
> *appointed a time for every matter.*
> *Ecclesiastes 3:13*

We have all heard or read of people who have done terrible things because of pain. This is a massive cost to our society to incarcerate or lose all that tremendous human potential in our world. We must work harder to solve our social problems and become a more compassionate and healthier civilization. Behind closed doors in some families are very dysfunctional individuals to whom society will pay a dear price. As in my own family, it was also amazing how many people became enablers of abusive people by not speaking out or excusing, ignoring, or even denying the behavior. I pray that we will learn how to better hold people accountable for the pain and destructive behavior they cause, especially to our children. We need to know new ways to recognize the sick before they hurt others.

Perhaps teaching forgiveness in school classes or through more evolving churches might be a path to healing those suffering before they injure others. This is a meaningful conversation, and we dearly need to create healthier societies.

Teachers and pastors gently guide us within the sacred walls of evolving churches, whispering the importance of forgiveness. The profound conversations that unfold, like delicate petals unfurling, nurture the seeds of compassion within those who suffer.

Through these shared experiences, our society permeates with a collective yearning for healing. We recognize the urgency of cultivating forgiveness to prevent further pain and injury. This transformative journey can forge healthier communities and foster understanding and empathy.

This conversation is not just a desire; it is a necessity. It is a call to action, a plea to weave forgiveness into the very fabric of our existence. Only then can we heal the wounds that afflict us and create a world where compassion and forgiveness fill our hearts.

Understanding evil in our world is complex, and finding forgiveness is just as tricky. Overcoming is to love better no matter what life throws at us, which takes great resolve. Sophie will need great love, and with God, I want to support her in every way I can.

Do not be overcome by evil, but overcome evil with good. And now abide faith, hope, love, these three: but the greatest of these is love. 1Corintheians 13:13

Today, I sat down to answer Sophie's second letter. She has indeed asked the most difficult question.

Dearest Darling Sophie,
I was so excited to receive
your beautiful letter. It is
such wonderful news that the
first surgery is done, and
you are recovering well.
While this is the first of two
surgeries, it is over, and I
am told it was very
successful. Doctors can do so
many amazing things.
Soon, this will all be behind
you and leave only
memories. As we discussed
before, no one deserves to be
attacked and physically

145

harmed. It is an evil act, and my heart breaks that this happened to you. You did not deserve this, nor did anyone. God has granted us all free will to make our own choices. God granted us this freedom and does not interfere with anyone's choices.

Unfortunately, we live in a world where some people make wrong choices. They make choices that cause harm or pain to someone else. While these terrible things happen, Jesus weeps and relives his crucifixion. He suffered terribly on the day of his crucifixion so we could be

forgiven for these evils or wrong
choices.

While Jesus promises we are
forgiven, he also promises God's
justice for those who commit
evil.

The Bible says in Romans
12:19

"Leave it to the wrath of God, for
it is written Vengeance is Mine.
I will repay." Says the lord.

In Romans 12:18, justice
assures us that all will
someday answer for what they
have done, and justice will be
administered. God is your
comfort. God can

heal your heart and mind as no
one else can.

The Lord is near to the
brokenhearted and saves the
crushed in spirit. Psalms 34:1
My favorite psalm is 23:4 Even
though I walk through the
valley of the shadow of death.
 I will fear no evil, for you are
with me.
Your rod and your staff they
comfort me.

Please understand that none of
this was your fault and that
God is in Charge. The courts
will do what the courts

do, and God will do the rest. Your job is to heal in body and mind and let the rest go. I am so happy you have wonderful friends and family all around you. They will be a great comfort to you. Please know I am with you in heart and prayer as our letters continue. We will all celebrate the healing joy you so dearly deserve. You are so beautiful and have great strength. Nothing and no one can ever take your beauty or soul from you.

In 1 Peter 3:4, the Bible says, " It is your unfading beauty of a gentle and quiet spirit

that is most precious to God." He
speaks of your beauty, Sophie.
God cherishes you just as he
cherishes all his children. I also
love your faith, courage,
friendship, and loved ones all
around you.

Suppose you see a bright blue
balloon with your name and a
note tucked inside with my
prayer for you. It is your
balloon, Sophie, that we set free
this morning to fly away and
touch the face of the heavens.
My family and I watched it
until it was out of view, and it
was a beautiful sight.

Wouldn't it be wonderful to see it? Even if you don't, it is gracing the heavens above you, carrying a prayer just for you.
Kisses and hugs, and warmest blessings always of Love.
Mary-Eisa

My prayer for Sophie.

Dearest God, I pray for the complete peace of Sophie's mind and soul.
May her body be healed and restored. May her doctors be guided with the wisdom to know exactly how best to help Sophie and, with God's love, see her healing complete.
May Sophie be healed to the perfection in which she was created whole and perfect in every way.

May she always be surrounded by love and peace as she continues her journey in life cautiously but without fear or anger towards anyone.

I pray this, dear Father, in your name and in the name of your son Jesus Christ, Amen.

Sophie and I still correspond, and it is a remarkable joy to see how beautiful her life is today. She has found her path to study medicine, which is a tribute to herself, her family, the world, and God.

Walking along
My shadow beside me
Watching the moon.
        –Sodo

Part Three
Prayers and Musings.

On Christmas Eve 1968, the astronauts said, "And, for all the people back on Earth, the crew of Apollo 8 have a message that we would like to send to you." And they began to read the biblical story of creation. "In the beginning, God created the heavens and the earth."

The story of creation beaming down to us on Christmas Eve, even the steely-eyed flight directors in Mission Control wept. The spirit of Apollo delivered a message of peace for all humankind.

From a young Canadian RAF pilot to John the Baptist and the Apollo 8 astronauts – each sought to reach out and touch the face of God. And now, it's our turn to reach out and touch the face of God. To stand in the presence of the holy one and leap for joy at the coming of Jesus as one of us – flesh of our flesh and bone of our bone.

155

A Flower Does Not Talk

Silently, a flower Blooms In silence, it falls away,
Yet here now, at this moment, at this place,
The whole of the flower, the whole of the world, is blooming.
This is the talk of the flower, the truth of the blossom:
The glory of eternal life is fully shining here.
–Zenkei Shibayama

Together in the Heart
is a
wonderful place
to Be.

Walking In Love

Dear God,

May I always walk in your footsteps of love,
And pray to be a light shining from your
glory,
May my heart always embrace your love,
And shine a light on all I meet.
May I be guided by your wisdom and feel
safe,
And enfolded in your peace.
May I never stray from the pureness of your
love.
May I be filled with your light, And always
be that light, Until you guide me home.
Amen.

Everything that has a beginning has an ending. Make your peace with that And all will be well

–Buddha

Every Day A Blessing

Good Morning, God, Thank you for this
day,

Thank you for all your blessings in my life.
I pray this morning for your love to fill up
my heart,

And flow to the hearts of every other soul.
I pray we live in a world together in peace
and love.

A world that is free of war.
Where we live together in harmony. A
planet created by you in love.

And So It Is..

Don't close the Book on life
When bad things happen
Just remember it is an
opportunity.
To paint a whole new canvas,
To begin a whole new Chapter.

Trees

I think that I shall never see
A poem as lovely as a tree.
A tree whose hungry mouth is prest Against the
earth's sweet flowing breast;
A tree that looks at God all day, And lifts her leafy
arms to pray; A tree that may, in Summer wear A
nest of robins in her hair;
Upon whose bosom snow has lain; Who
intimately lives with rain, Poems are made by
fools like me, But only God can make a tree.
–Joyce Kilmer

Looking at things in a new way
Allows you to see things
All new and
Differently.

Breathing In Love

My body flows with love, Flowing as a river
of love.
I am like the swells of the ocean bursting
through a valley,
I rise in and out as with the breath of God.
From the highest mountain to the lowest
creek,
I wish to flow as currents of love.
To be cleansed by the pristine waters from
heaven above.
And feel God's vibration and eternal spark.
Filling me with health, radiance, and love.
Amen.

The way I see it is you want
to see the rainbow
You have to put up
with the rain.
–Dolly Parton

Wholeness

Dear God, Take from me my pain.
Allow my body to be healed.
May every cell of my being
radiate in love.
From the top of my head to
the toes of my feet.
May my body flow within God's light.
Healed and perfect.
In every way,
Thank you, God
So It Is. Amen.

All the Inspiration
And knowledge of the world
Can't help
Until you are ready to accept
And ask for help.

Lost My Way

Dear God, today I lost my way and
fell into despair.
Another's words cut into
my heart.
While my tears flowed like rain.
Suddenly, I felt your love all
around me.
As your hands gathered up my tears.
I knew no words could ever
harm me again.
With a grateful heart. Amen.

Everything that is
to be Created
Must first begin in
The mind.
As all creation must
First, begin,
There.

Keep My Child Safe

Dear God, I pray my child and all children
are safe at school.
As children travel to school, I pray
they arrive safely.
I pray for the teachers to be guided
in caring for every child. May the children
and teachers have safe and kind days.
I pray for God's angels to surround and
bless all the children and schools.
This is my prayer for all our children.
And so, it is now and forever.

Amen

Joined Together

Today, I will be united in marriage,
Creating our union of love. As we begin our
joyful path together.
May each day make our bond stronger.
And without exception, behold the light in
each other, and, may the universe always
bless and smile upon us.
While the joy in our hearts continues
forever.
Amen

It's a New Year!
Time to smile much bigger
Laugh a little louder
Find more to give
And even more to forgive.
Love with all your heart
Sing the songs of praise
And dance the dance of Joy

Safety in a World of Chaos

Dear God, I do not feel safe in our
world, which is so chaotic.
I pray for a future built on love, not hate
 and violence.
Safe for family and home.
A world with enjoyable work.
In a work environment that is caring
 and pleasant.
I want to do loving things in my world.
To see dreams become a reality, I will
 place them all with you.
Thank you for my life, my dreams, and
you.
Amen

Be grateful for all those you can love.
And for every second, you have to do
it.
Life is so precious that if you spend it
Blessing all those you love.
Every day will be like a magical gift.

Loving Myself

I choose to see myself as God sees
me.
Whole, Beautiful, and Free. I
accept that I am created in God's
perfection.
Precisely as God wished me to be.

Amen

God Took Home My Loved One

I know your love is now always with
(name of loved one)
Keeping them safe while the angels
guide (him/her) home.
To the place where there is only love.
As I let go of any fear, knowing (he/she)
is in your loving care.
Trusting they are eternally safe.
With memories safely in my heart. Our
love is like a cord that binds us together.

And will never break.

Love is eternal, and our bond is
eternal.

Until we meet again.

Amen

My Pet Has Passed

Dear God,
Today, my best friend passed into your
love.
My heart is broken, and I miss my
(name of pet)
I loved that furry (feathered)
friend with all my heart.
The love and comfort returned to me
were endless.
God, please care for my dearly loved
friend.
Keep my friend safe as you do all your
creatures.
Until we can share another hug and I
meet my best friend again.
Amen

Loving Myself as God Loves Me

May I see myself as God sees me.
And trust in God's vision to guide me
in all I do.
To be a blessing in this world,
loving and caring.
Trusting always in those who
guide my ways.
To be guided as God would want. To
see me safely in life and journey.
Blessed always in God's love.
Amen

For God so loved the world that

he gave his

*Only son, that whoever
believes in him should not
perish but have eternal life.
John 3:16*

My Work Dear God,

 May the work I do always be a blessing.

May I enrich my work and be a blessing to
my co-workers.

As we all prosper and are guided to do good
and loving work.

I pray that management will be guided by
wisdom and love. I am grateful for this
loving work that I do.

Amen

You are Kind

You are smart

You are so beautiful

You are strength

And you are my friend.

Protection

I pray for God's love all around me.

As I drive on the roads and live my
life at home.

As I enjoy every day and all that I do.

May the angels always surround me
and be my guidance and protection
everywhere I am.

May my loved ones always be safe
and our journeys in life surrounded
by angels.

As I pray for love and protection
wherever I go.

And so it is.

Amen.

God has four gifts for you

A solution for every problem

A light for every dark shadow

A hand to guide your steps

Peace placed in your heart.

Walk A Better Way

Dear God,
My life has been full of strife and
turbulence.
Please help me walk a better way.
May I see your light in all that I do.
And may your light guide my
steps along my way.
May I walk without fear, and be
stronger every day. Richer in
heart and soul.
Free from unconscious conflict. I am
able to help my fellow men and
sisters.

To always walk with you.
As I pray to walk a better way.
Amen

To Know My Worth

When I feel unloved and unworthy of
 love

 In my moment of despair, I pray to

 feel your hand.

A hand to lift me up and stand me tall.

 It is a hand I desperately need.

A hand to embrace me in a world

 I feel lost in.

A world you left in such a painful way.

 To give me a world to live in.

A world filled with trees, flowers, and
 birds that sing.

A beauty to remind us that you never left.

 Everything is of you, as I am too.

Dear God, guide me through these

moments to lift me to hope and never
despair again.

And so, it is.

Amen.

About the Author

Mary-Eisa grew up in New England and enjoys writing about her marvelous exploration of Massachusetts and Maine through her books.

Immerse yourself in the world of a brilliant author whose love for nature, prayer, and God is the source of her inspiration. Her life story is a healing melody that moves you to your core. With her global prayer work, she spreads hope and devotion, filling the air with sweet scents that will make your heart sing. Each word she writes is a journey that will inspire you to experience the warmth and beauty of faith. Her work reminds us that the Universe is present in every aspect of our lives and that we are surrounded by a tapestry of sights, sounds, and feelings illuminating our existence and purpose. Get ready to be swept away by her captivating story!

BIBLIOGRAPHY

Mahmud Shabistan 14th century Poet. Hua-Yen Buddhism, The Jewel of Indra by Francis H. Cook

Elizabeth Barret Browning, a Victorian poet (1806- 1861) excerpt from poem Aurora Leigh

Ralph Waldo Emerson, a 19th-century American essayist, lecturer, and poet. (1803-1882)

Henry David Thoreau, a 19th-century American naturalist, essayist, and poet. (1817-1872)

Jalaluddin Rumi, a 13th century Persian poet, Sufi mystic. (1207-1273)

Albert Einstein, German born theoretical physicist, (1879-1955)

Gandhi Indian lawyer, nationalist, political ethicist. (1869-1948)

Carl Gustav Jung, Swiss Psychiatrist, Psychoanalyst, (1875-1961)

Surah Al-Waq, Qur'an verses 56-71

189

Angelus Silesius, German Catholic priest, physician, mystic, religious poet. (1624- 1677)

St. John of the Cross, Spanish Catholic priest, Mystic. (1542-1591)

Mahmud Shabistan 14th century Poet. Hua- Yen Buddhism, The Jewel of Indra by Francis H. Cook

Elizabeth Barret Browning, a Victorian poet (1806- 1861) excerpt from poem Aurora Leigh

Ralph Waldo Emerson, a 19th-century American essayist, lecturer, and poet. (1803- 1882)

Henry David Thoreau, a 19th-century American naturalist, essayist, and poet. (1817-1872)

Jalaluddin Rumi, a 13th century Persian poet, Sufi mystic. (1207-1273)

Albert Einstein, German born theoretical physicist, (1879-1955)

Gandhi Indian lawyer, nationalist, political

ethicist. (1869-1948)

Carl Gustav Jung, Swiss Psychiatrist, Psychoanalyst, (1875-1961)

Surah Al-Waq, Qur'an verses 56-71

Angelus Silesius, German Catholic priest,
physician, mystic, religious poet. (1624- 1677)

St. John of the Cross, Spanish Catholic priest,
Mystic. (1542-1591)

To the many, I wish to acknowledge this book. It is with such gratitude that I have been blessed to write from the heart and through the imagination of nature and everyone who has participated in this life journey. If there are stories to tell, it is because of the impressions received from all those beautiful beings about our everyday lives. Thank you.

I am available at: www. mary-eisa.com

The **mary-eisa@mary-eisa.com**

This is my ministry, where I have continued my work worldwide. It is a joy to help and work with others who need a bright moment. I cannot solve people's problems, but I can maybe add a ray of light and prayer to assist anyone I can.

www.ingramcontent.com/pod-product-compliance
Lightning Source LLC
Chambersburg PA
CBHW051519120626
46551CB00012B/987